DATE DUE			

13FL03929

303.48
COM

Computers and technology

Computers and Technology

SCIENCE NEWS for KIDS

SCIENCE
NEWS
for
KIDS

Computers and Technology

Series Editor
Tara Koellhoffer

With a Foreword by
Emily Sohn,
Science News for Kids

CHELSEA
CLUBHOUSE
An Imprint of Chelsea House Publishers

Computers and Technology

Chelsea Clubhouse
An imprint of Chelsea House Publishers
132 West 31st Street
New York NY 10001

For Library of Congress Cataloging-in-Publication Data, please contact the publisher.

ISBN 0-7910-9120-1

Chelsea House books are available at special discounts when purchased in bulk quantities for businesses, associations, institutions, or sales promotions. Please call our Special Sales Department in New York at (212) 967-8800 or (800) 322-8755.

You can find Chelsea House on the World Wide Web at
http://www.chelseahouse.com

Text and cover design by Takeshi Takahashi
Layout by Ladybug Editorial & Design

Printed in the United States of America

Bang   10 9 8 7 6 5 4 3 2 1

This book is printed on acid-free paper.

All links, web addresses, and Internet search terms were checked and verified to be correct at the time of publication. Because of the dynamic nature of the web, some addresses and links may have changed since publication and may no longer be valid.

Contents Overview

Detailed Table of Contents

Detailed Table of Contents

by Emily Sohn
Science News for Kids

Science, for many kids, is just another subject in school. You may have biology tests and astronomy quizzes to study for, chemistry formulas to memorize, physics problems to work through, or current events to report on. All of it, after a while, can seem like a major drag.

Now, forget about all that, and think about your day. What did you eat for breakfast? How did you get to school and what did you think about along the way? What makes the room bright enough for you to see this book? How does the room stay cool or warm enough for you to be comfortable? What do you like to do for fun?

All of your answers, in some way, involve science. Food, transportation, electricity, toys, video games, animals, plants, your brain, the rest of your body: Behind the scenes of nearly anything you can think of, there are scientists trying to figure out how it works, how it came to be, or how to make it better. Science can explain why pizza and chocolate taste good. Science gives airplanes a lift. And science is behind the medicines that make your aches and pains go away. Most exciting of all, science never stands still.

Science News for Kids tracks the trends and delves into the discoveries that make life more interesting and more efficient every day. The stories in these volumes explore a tiny fraction of the grand scope of research happening around the world. These stories point out the questions that push scientists to probe ever deeper into physics, chemistry, biology, psychology, and more. Reading about the challenges of science will spark in you the same sort of curiosity that drives researchers to keep searching for answers, despite setbacks and failed experiments. The stories here may even inspire you to seek out your own solutions to the world's puzzles.

Being a scientist is hard work, but it can be one of the best jobs around. You may picture scientists always tinkering away in their labs, pouring chemicals into flasks and reading technical papers. Well, they do those things some of the time. But they also get to dig around in the dirt, blow things up, and even ride rockets into outer space. They travel around the world. They save lives. And, they get to spend most of their time thinking about the things that fascinate them most, all in the name of work.

Sometimes, researchers have revelations that change the way we think about the universe. Albert Einstein, for one, explained light, space, time, and other aspects of the physical world in radically new terms. He's perhaps the most famous scientist in history, thanks to his theories of relativity and other ideas. Likewise, James Watson and

Francis Crick forever changed the face of medicine when they first described the structure of the genetic material DNA in 1953. Today, doctors use information about DNA to explain why some people are likely to develop certain diseases and why others may have trouble reading or doing math. Police investigators rely on DNA to solve mysteries when they analyze hairs, blood, saliva, and remains at the scene of a crime. And scientists are now eagerly pursuing potential uses of DNA to cure cancer and other diseases.

Science can be about persistence and courage as much as it is about grand ideas. Society doesn't always welcome new ideas. Before Galileo Galilei became one of the first people to point a telescope at the sky in the early 1600s, for example, nearly everyone believed that the planets revolved around Earth. Galileo discovered four moons orbiting Jupiter. He saw that Venus has phases, like the moon. And he noticed spots on the sun and lumps on the moon's craggy face. All of these observations shook up the widely held view that the heavens were perfect, orderly, and centered on Earth. Galileo's ideas were so controversial, in fact, that he was forced to deny them to save his life. Even then, he was sentenced to imprisonment in his own home.

Since Galileo's time, the public has so completely accepted his views of the universe that space missions have been named after him, as have craters on the moon and on Mars. In 1969, Neil Armstrong became the first person to stand on the moon. Now, astronauts spend months in orbit, living on an international space station, floating in weightlessness. Spacecraft have landed on planets and moons as far away as Saturn. One probe recently slammed into a comet to collect information. With powerful telescopes, astronomers continue to spot undiscovered moons in our solar system, planets orbiting stars in other parts of our galaxy, and evidence of the strange behavior of black holes. New technologies continue to push the limits of what we can detect in outer space and what we know about how the universe formed.

Here on Earth, computer technology has transformed society in a short period of time. The first electronic digital computers, which appeared in the 1940s, took up entire rooms and weighed thousands of pounds. Decades passed before people started using their own PCs (personal computers) at home. Laptops came even later.

These days, it's hard to imagine life without computers. They track restaurant orders. They help stores process credit cards. They allow you to play video games, send e-mails and instant messages to your friends, and write reports that you can edit and print without ever picking up a pen. Doctors use computers to diagnose their patients, and banks use computers to keep track of our money. As computers become more and more popular, they continue to get smaller, more powerful, less expensive, and more integrated into our lives in ways we don't even notice.

Probes that fly to Pluto and computers the size of peas are major advances that don't happen overnight. Science is a process of small steps, and a new discovery often starts with a single question. Why, for example, do hurricanes and tsunamis form? What is it like at the center of Earth? Why do some types of french fries taste better than others? Research projects can also begin with observations. There are fewer tigers in India than there used to be, for instance. Kids now weigh more than they did a generation ago. Mars shows signs that the planet once supported life.

The next step is investigation, which can take on many forms, depending on the subject. Brain researchers, for one, often do experiments in their laboratories with the help of sophisticated equipment. In one type of neuroscience study, subjects repeatedly solve tasks while machines measure activity in their brains. Some environmental scientists who study climate, on the other hand, collect data by tracking weather patterns over the years. Paleontologists dig deep into the earth to look for clues about what the world was like when dinosaurs were alive. Anthropologists learn about other cultures by talking to people and collecting stories. Doctors monitor large numbers of patients taking a new drug or no drug to figure out whether a drug is safe and effective before others can use it.

Designing studies requires creativity, and scientists spend many years training to use the tools of their profession. Physicists need to learn complicated mathematical formulas. Ecologists make models that simulate interactions between species. Physicians learn the name of every bone and blood vessel in the body. The most basic tools, however, are ones that everyone has: our senses. The best way to start learning about the world through science is to pay attention to what you smell, taste, see, hear, and feel. Notice. Ask questions. Collect data. Do experiments. Draw tentative conclusions. Ask more questions.

Most importantly, leave no stone unturned. There's no limit to the topics available for research. Robots, computers, and new technologies in medicine are the waves of the future. Just as important, however, are studies of the past. Figuring out what Earth's climate used to be like and which animals and plants used to live here are the first steps toward understanding how the planet is changing and what those changes might mean for our future. And don't forget to look around at what's going on around you, right now. You might just be surprised at how many subjects you can find to investigate.

Ready to get started? The stories in this book are great sources of inspiration. Each of the articles comes directly from the *Science News for Kids* Website, which you can find online at *http://sciencenewsforkids.org*. All articles at the site, which is updated weekly, cover current events in science, and all are written with middle-school students in mind. If anything you read in this book sparks your interest, feel free to visit the Website to check out the latest developments and find out more.

And keep an eye out for an occasional feature called "News Detective." These essays describe what it's like to be a science journalist, roaming the world in search of scientists at work. Science writing is an often-overlooked career possibility, but science writers have endless opportunities to learn about many things at once, to share in the excitement of scientific discovery, and to help scientists get the word out about the significance of their work.

So, go ahead and turn the page. There's so much left to discover.

Section 1

Computers

The world has changed a lot in the last 50 years. For almost a century, the telephone stood out as perhaps the greatest innovation in the history of communication. By the end of the 20th century, computers had changed communication—not to mention transportation, medicine, and all other aspects of life and commerce—forever.

Today, you can find computers in every business, classroom, and even most homes. We use them to work, to play, to learn, and to stay in touch with people. Through e-mail and instant messaging, you can send a note to a friend at the click of a mouse button, and the Internet has opened up new ways to meet people and spend your free time. Many of us can hardly imagine living in a world without computers. In this section, we look at some of the latest advances in the computer industry and find out how new technology may make computers even more useful in our daily lives.

The first article explores the idea of interactive computers that would be able to respond not only to the moves you make with the keyboard and mouse, but also to your mood. By means of sensors and sophisticated software, these new computers would be more like friends than just machines. The second article describes the linguistic changes that have evolved along with the widespread use of e-mail and instant messaging. Although some experts worry that today's young people are not learning to write and speak properly, others argue that online "slang" is just a natural change in the way we speak—the kind of change that might occur even if we weren't using computers. Next, we examine the increasing use of virtual reality technology to make education accessible to everyone. Finally, in the last article of the section. we learn about the development of "electronic paper," which may someday make printed books obsolete.

—The Editor

Your Friend,
the Computer

Most of us use our computers to stay in touch with our friends, but what if the computer itself was your friend? Right now, scientists are hard at work trying to make that idea a reality. It's possible that with the right combination of sophisticated sensors, your computer would be able to notice even the slightest changes in your body temperature or stress level and respond in a way that makes you feel better. This "sensitive" computer would be able to keep track of the events going on in your life and congratulate you when something great happened or console you when you felt down. This article by Sorcha McDonagh delves in the science of interactive computing.

—The Editor

Computers With Attitude

by Sorcha McDonagh

Before Reading:

- **What would you like to change about computers to make them better?**

- **Name a movie or story in which a computer has a personality.**

It's been a long day at school. You've got a heavy evening of homework ahead. You switch on your computer to work on an assignment. An animated kid on your computer screen smiles and says, "Hey, it's good to see you again. But you look tired. Are you doing OK?"

You reply that you're feeling pretty wiped out, but you've got a research project to do. You rub your eyes and yawn. "I know the feeling," your computer-kid replies, blinking and sighing. "But don't worry. We'll get through it together in no time."

If a friendly, caring computer like this sounds far-fetched to you, think again.

Computer scientists and engineers are busy trying to design computers that can recognize how you're feeling.

The computers would then offer help or just a little friendly company while you work or play.

But it may be years before you'll have a computer that can tell when you're bored and respond by telling you a joke. Or a computer that cheers you on and gives you hints when you're feeling frustrated with a math problem.

KEYBOARD OR MOUSE

Think about how you interact with your computer now. You can type on a keyboard or click a mouse. Maybe you can also pound on a joypad, press on a touch screen, or even speak into a microphone.

The computer has no idea when you're frustrated with it. It can't tell whether you're bored or entertained. When it comes to how you're feeling, your computer hasn't got a clue.

This severely limits a computer's ability to help you, says Winslow Burleson. He's a student at the Massachusetts Institute of Technology (MIT).

Burleson is one of many computer scientists who predict that computers someday will recognize human emotions and respond to them.

This idea belongs to a field in computer science known as "sensitive computing" or "affective computing." The word *affective* refers to anything related to emotions.

COMPUTER BUDDIES

For a computer to sense your feelings, it needs more input than just your stroke on a keyboard or your movement of a mouse. Ideally, an affective computer would hear, see, and even touch its users, says computer scientist Rosalind Picard.

Such a computer needs sensors, such as cameras and microphones. It must then interpret what it senses. What does a smile or frown mean? How does your tone of voice suggest whether you're excited, angry, or bored?

At MIT's Affective Computing Lab, Picard and her students are building several systems that can do some of these things. One is called the Learning Companion. It's a software buddy that can be added to educational programs, such as quizzes and lessons.

The Learning Companion generates an animated character—a kid—on the computer screen. The screen kid helps you out with whatever problem you're working on.

"Right now, the character can smile, look at you, wave hello and good-bye," Burleson says. "It can jump up and down in excitement or in a frustrated tantrum."

Burleson predicts that, eventually, this virtual kid will

- **Why does Winslow Burleson want to design a computer that senses feelings and has emotions?**

- **What does "affective computing" mean?**

use input from sensors to tell whether you're paying attention. It'll also respond to your changing mood as you work at the computer. It'll know when to step in to help and when to stand by and let you keep working on your own.

A COMPUTER'S SENSES

The current version of the Learning Companion uses five different sensors to learn about a student sitting at a computer.

- **What is the Learning Companion?**

Two sensors are cameras. One camera focuses on your face, tracking changes that can show how you're feeling. For example, are you biting your lip or laughing? The second camera tracks what you're looking at to learn what's holding your attention. It might be a something on the screen or a person on the other side of the room.

The computer's mouse has a pressure sensor. Clicking the mouse really hard or over and over again can be a sign of frustration, Burleson explains.

A skin sensor detects how much your hands are sweating. Sweaty palms may indicate anxiety. The fifth sensor checks your posture. Are you on the edge of your seat or slouching?

But here's where things get complicated. A student's

posture by itself doesn't necessarily indicate interest or boredom. Some kids slouch even when they're engrossed in what they're doing. And a frown doesn't always mean frustration. For some kids, it might mean they're just busy thinking about a puzzle.

- **What sorts of sensors could provide data to a computer so that it could figure out how you're feeling?**

You can usually tell how a friend is feeling by watching her face or listening to the tone of her voice.

Attention Gamers!

Do you play a great science fiction-based video or computer game? Do you know it really well?

Just like movies, games have writers as well. In fact, many role-playing games have a team of writers who create their complex settings and elaborate action. Some of the most fascinating games to play have an underlying story. And—you guessed it—if it's a science fiction story, it has science at its core.

The next time you play this game, pay attention to the story and its setting. What is the underlying problem that must be solved to win the game? How is science involved in it? Or is science more important in the setting or the technology?

- **How could this technology change your MP3 player or your cell phone?**

Evaluating a combination of signals automatically comes naturally to you. Teaching a computer to do the same thing is difficult. That's what Burleson and his colleagues are working on.

FUTURE COMPANIONS

What might a Learning Companion of the future be like?

"A lot of things we see in science fiction might become available," Burleson says. "There could be peer robots that play with you, enhancing your abilities and your creativity."

Picard has suggested that computer games could monitor how scared you are and award extra points for brave game-play.

It's not just computers that may become buddies. How about an MP3 player that senses when you're feeling stressed and selects music to calm you down? Or a cell phone that knows you just got some great news and automatically dials your best friend's number?

- **What problems does this article suggest might arise from a computer that tries to sense your emotions and react to them?**

For Picard, the biggest question isn't whether it's possible for computers to do all these things. It's whether people will be ready to deal with them when they do.

Will you?

After Reading:

- Would you want to use a computer that senses your feelings and responds to them? Why or why not?

- What other signs besides the ones listed in that article might suggest that a kid is losing interest in something?

- In the movies, there are examples of computers with emotions that turn out to be evil. Why do you think people might be afraid of computers with emotions?

- Do you think you would learn better from a human teacher or a computer tutor? What are the advantages and disadvantages of each?

Going Deeper:

Sohn, Emily. "What Video Games Can Teach Us." *Science News for Kids* (January 21, 2004). Available online at *http://www.sciencenewsforkids.org/articles/20040121/Feature1.asp*.

Is Instant Messaging Changing Our Language?

Instant messages are a great way to keep in touch with your friends, especially if you're already working on your computer, but you may have noticed that the way you "talk" over the Internet is very different from the way you talk in person. And it's not just because you're typing your words. After all, don't you write very differently when you hand in an essay in school from how you write a quick IM to a friend? Some experts are worried about the increasing use of Internet "slang"—the shortcuts and abbreviations we use so we can type faster and keep the online conversation going. This article by Emily Sohn looks at the new "language" of instant messages and the effects it's having on the way people communicate all over the world.

—The Editor

The Snappy Lingo of Instant Messages

by Emily Sohn

Before Reading:

- **What is instant messaging?**

- **Give three examples of shortcuts or abbreviations that kids might use in an e-mail or text message to save having to spell out the entire phrase.**

The following is part of an actual conversation between two college students, Gale and Sally.

> Gale: hey I gotta run
> Sally: Okay.
> Sally: I'll ttyl?
> Gale: gotta do errands.
> Gale: yep!!
> Sally: Okay.
> Sally: :-)
> Gale: talk to you soon
> Sally: Alrighty.

It would sound silly to say these words out loud, and you wouldn't write like this in a school report. Still, the conversation made perfect sense when Gale and Sally fired it off to each other on their computers.

The young women were having an instant messaging (IM) conversation. Each person could see what the other was writing every time one of them pressed the "return" key, even though they were in different places.

Now, scientists are studying instant messaging, cell phone text messages, and e-mails to try to understand how technology is changing the way we communicate (Figure 1.1). The research belongs to a field called linguistics, the scientific study of language.

CHANGING LANGUAGE

Change is a natural part of language development. The words you like to use are probably a little different from those that your grandparents used when they were young. Reading a play by William Shakespeare shows how much language can change in 400 years.

- **How does instant messaging differ from e-mail?**

Nonetheless, some language experts worry about the future of languages. They cringe when people break the rules of grammar, fail to use proper punctuation, misuse a word, or even invent a new one just for fun. They don't like the way slang words and pop phrases creep into the way we write and speak.

Another worry is that computers are speeding up the spread of English around the globe and forcing people to neglect their native languages. Like some species, languages have been dying out at an alarming rate, and some linguists fear that the Internet might be partially to blame.

Another group of researchers, however, is fascinated by the interaction between language and the Internet. Instead of killing languages, the rapid rise of Internet communication has opened up an exciting new branch of linguistics, says David Crystal. He's a linguist at the University of Wales in Bangor.

"We should be exulting, in fact, that the Internet is allowing us to explore language in a creative way," Crystal says. "This is a new branch of study. Like no other study of language change in history, it allows us to follow the rate of change of grammar, pronunciation, and vocabulary."

COMPUTER TALK

Researchers now have a name for instant messages, cell phone text messages, and e-mail. They call it **computer-mediated communication**, or CMC.

CMC is different from speech in a number of ways, Crystal says. There's no immediate feedback to an e-mail, for one thing. You can have multiple IM or e-mail conversations at once, which you can't have when you're talking directly to people. And on the computer, you lose

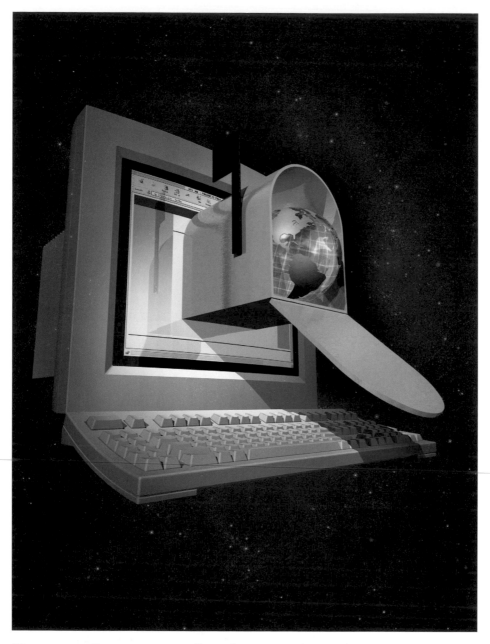

Figure 1.1 Computer-mediated communication—through e-mail, text messages, and instant messaging—is dramatically changing language.

the effect of emotion and tone of voice, no matter how many smiley faces you use.

Computer messages are also different from normal writing. You can edit e-mails by cutting and pasting. You can add links. And you can get responses more quickly than you would from a letter.

All of these developments have led to the most rapid change in language since the Middle Ages, Crystal says. He encourages teachers to embrace the technology and its creative possibilities rather than fight against the trend.

Language shortcuts such "ttyl" (which means "talk to you later") obviously have no place in school reports, but events like text-messaging poetry competitions can be educational and fun. A British newspaper named *The Guardian*, for example, offers cash prizes to readers who come up with text message poems, using 160 characters or less.

MEN VERSUS WOMEN

Studying IM conversations can also be an interesting way to learn more about culture, relationships, and differences between men and women, says Naomi Baron. She's a linguist at American University in Washington, D.C.

In one study, Baron analyzed 23 IM conversations

between college students (including the one at the beginning of this article). In total, there were 2,185 transmissions and 11,718 words. She was surprised by what her data turned up.

For one thing, the messages were far less sloppy than she expected. Students seemed to be careful about what they wrote, and they tended to correct their mistakes. In fact, she says, students seemed to pay more attention to what they said in messages than they did in papers submitted for grading.

There were also major differences between men and women in how they used IM technology. Men tended to write in short phrases, while women tended to write in complete sentences. Women also took longer to say good-bye to each other.

Baron concluded that messaging between women is more like writing than speech. Messaging between men is more like speech than writing.

From questionnaires, Baron learned that most young people have between 1 and 12 IM conversations going on at once. "I couldn't imagine just having one IM conversation," one student said. "That would just be too weird." Before the invention of CMC, having that many conversations at once would have been practically impossible.

These patterns suggest that IM is something completely new in the history of communication, Baron says.

"I think we're entering a new era," she says, "in the way we think about speech and writing and how much control we have over the level at which we wish to interact and what kind of style we use."

• What surprised Naomi Baron about the IM messages that she studied?

INTERNET ACTIVITY

In recent years, the rise in the use of Internet communication has been greatest among young people. And the United States accounts for 20% of all Internet activity, says Brenda Danet. She's a researcher at Yale University in Connecticut and Hebrew University in Jerusalem.

Still, more and more people of all ages are using the Internet for longer stretches of time in countries around the world, especially in places such as China. And non-native English speakers make up at least two-thirds of Internet users, Danet says.

Nevertheless, her research has shown that English is used most of the time on international mailing lists because it's the language that most people have at least some knowledge of. The size and structure of keyboards also makes it particularly difficult to write in languages such as Chinese, Japanese, and Arabic.

- **Why is English so widely used on the Internet?**

- **What fraction of all Internet users are non-native English speakers?**

The wide use of English online makes many linguists worry that people are neglecting their own languages and abandoning their own cultures.

It's also true, however, that the Internet has opened up an explosion of possibilities for rapid communication across cultures. It might also be a good forum for the preservation of disappearing languages.

"Is the Internet contributing to the extinction of languages, or can it help revitalize them?" Danet asks. Only time will tell.

- **What is linguistics?**

SECRET NOTES

In the meantime, computer-mediated communication seems to be here to stay, says communications researcher Simeon Yates of Sheffield Hallam University.

The more we use IM, text messaging on our cell phones, and other new technologies, he says, the more they shape our lives and relationships.

People can now manage their schedules from anywhere and change plans at the last minute. They can send secret notes to each other over their phones without making a sound. People have even discovered ways to get across complicated feelings and emotions in only a few words.

A few generations ago, no one could have imagined that we would be communicating over computers in real time without ever speaking a word, Yates says. Now, people feel helpless without their e-mail and cell phones.

"This is basically your social life," Yates says. "When I ask British college students what they would do if I took their cell phones away, they say they couldn't live without them."

New technologies may open up additional communication possibilities in the future.

So, keep typing away. Just remember that technology shapes you every time you use it. And that could be a good thing or a bad thing, depending on how you look at it.

yup. OK 4 now. C U soon. ttyl!!!

After Reading:

- What is a blog? How might the widespread use of blogs change communication and the language people use to communicate with each other? See *www.techcentralstation.com/ 102704E.html* (*Tech Station Central*) or *www.businessweek.com/the_thread/techbeat/ archives/00000040.htm* (*Business Week*).

- Why do you think young people feel more comfortable with IM than many older people do?

- What are the pros and cons of the introduction of slang words into the English language?

- With typed words, it's hard to convey emotion. How might computers in the future help allow the expression or communication of emotion? See *www.aaai.org/AITopics/html/emotion.html* (*American Association for Artificial Intelligence*).

- Why do you think IM and Internet communication lend themselves to the development and use of slang?

Going Deeper:

To learn more about David Crystal and language development via the Internet, see *www.bangor.ac.uk/news/Crystal.htm*.

You can learn how instant messaging works online at *http://computer.howstuffworks.com/ instant-messaging.htm*.

The Virtual Classroom

You've probably heard of virtual reality technology, but you may think it's used mainly for ultra-realistic games or to train soldiers for combat. What if virtual reality could make it possible for you to go to school without ever leaving the comforts of home? The following article by Emily Sohn examines the ongoing development of a "Virtual Classroom," a method of bringing learning to students wherever they might be, as well as a possible way to help kids who are easily distracted by the busy environment in a real school get a better education.

—The Editor

A Classroom of the Mind

by Emily Sohn

Before Reading:

- **What kinds of technology imitate reality in some way?**

- **Why might someone want to imitate a classroom?**

- **Name some things that often distract you from your schoolwork. Are there other things that help you concentrate?**

You're sitting at your desk. A teacher is writing on the chalkboard. A bus rumbles past the window. Kids are yelling on the playground outside. A paper airplane whizzes overhead. The school principal steps into the room, looks around, and walks out. A book falls off the desk next to you. Suddenly, the teacher hands you a pop quiz.

Don't panic! You aren't actually in school. You're in a "virtual classroom." Everything you see and hear is coming to you through a computer-operated display that you're wearing on your head like a pair of very bulky goggles.

Unlike the classroom, the technology is real. It's an innovative application of **virtual reality**, a type of technology that uses computer programs to simulate real-world (or even fantasy) situations. Wearing virtual-reality gear, you can find yourself sitting in a classroom, touring a famous museum, wandering across a weird landscape, zooming into space, or playing with a cartoon character. You don't have to leave your room.

- **What is virtual reality? Who typically uses it?**

Movie directors and video game producers have been using computers for years to create ever more realistic special effects. Some companies are now building three-dimensional fantasy worlds in which players, linked by computer networks, appear to meet and go on quests together. Virtual-reality gear that delivers images and sounds directly to your eyes and ears makes these fake worlds seem lifelike.

Some psychologists are also getting into the act. They see virtual reality technology as a useful tool for learning more about why people act as they do. It could help psychologists better identify and come up with solutions for behavior problems, for example.

"We've spent the last 100 years looking for certain laws in how people interact with the real world," says clinical psychologist Albert "Skip" Rizzo. "Now, we've got a powerful tool that lets us create worlds, control things, and see how people perform. This is a psychologist's dream."

Gavit Middle/High School
1670 175th Street
Hammond, IN 46324

- **Why have psychologists started to see virtual reality as a useful tool?**

Rizzo works in the school of engineering at the University of Southern California in Los Angeles, where he developed the Virtual Classroom and a related program called the Virtual Office.

VIRTUAL CLASSROOM

Some kids can't sit still for long. They have a hard time paying attention to just one thing. They're easily distracted. They can get very impatient. They hate standing in line or waiting for their turn in a game or activity. They get bored pretty fast. They may also be impulsive—saying the first thing that comes to mind or interrupting someone else who's talking.

For certain kids, this problem is so severe that doctors have a name for it: **attention-deficit/hyperactivity disorder**, or ADHD. Perhaps as many as 1 out of every 20 kids under the age of 18 have characteristics of ADHD. Often, these kids have trouble getting through school and face other difficulties later in life.

Rizzo started developing the Virtual Classroom in 1999. He wanted to see if he could use it as a tool for testing and treating kids who have attention disorders.

To diagnose ADHD, doctors typi-

- **What is ADHD? What are some of its symptoms?**

cally test patients by giving them tasks that require attention. As part of one classic test, you watch letters flashed on a computer screen. Every time you see the letter "A" followed by the letter "X," you have to press the space bar. If you're paying close attention, you'll register all the times this combination occurs. If not, you'll miss some.

The Virtual Classroom makes these tests more efficient, Rizzo says. In one experiment, he gave a group of kids the classic "A-X" test. Instead of looking at a computer screen in a doctor's office, though, the kids wore headsets that made it look like they were taking the test in a classroom.

"Basically what we found," Rizzo says, "is that, in 20 minutes of testing with virtual reality, we replicated a finding that usually requires a couple hours of standard testing with computer screens in the psychologist's office."

REALISTIC FEATURES

Encouraged by these results, Rizzo and his colleagues started programming additional features into their Virtual Classroom. Introducing distractions was one of them.

Even though teachers try their best to keep their classrooms quiet and orderly, real life can get pretty chaotic. So, the researchers added people

- **To test kids for ADHD, how might the Virtual Classroom be better than classic A-X tests?**

walking around, noises coming from the hallway, paper airplanes flying every which way, and other distractions.

When Rizzo tested kids with and without ADHD using the more advanced program, he found some interesting patterns. Even without distractions, kids with ADHD performed worse on the "A-X" task than did kids without attention problems. When they had to deal with distractions at the same time, the differences between the two groups were even more striking, Rizzo says.

Because the Virtual Classroom more accurately mimics real life, diagnoses become more reliable than with traditional testing methods, Rizzo says. He thinks his program could reduce the number of kids who take Ritalin® and other medications for ADHD because it does a better job of identifying the most serious problems.

The next step will be to move from diagnoses to treatments. Spending time in a carefully controlled Virtual Classroom might help train kids to pay better attention, even when facing the multitude of distractions that confront them every day.

That may be the only way psychology will ever keep pace with modern society, Rizzo says.

INFORMATION DELUGE

"We're living in an information deluge," he says. "One person estimated that a Sunday edition of the *New York*

Times contains more information than a person was exposed to in an entire lifetime in the 18th century." And there's a lot more around than just the Sunday newspaper.

- **How might the Virtual Classroom be used to treat kids with ADHD?**

Kids are growing up in an increasingly high-tech, computer-dominated world. "We're not going to entice this generation of kids in the classroom or later in job training with old, traditional tools," Rizzo says. "Their brains are wired for speed. You can complain about that all you want, but this is reality."

Grownups, too, stand a chance of benefiting from virtual reality technology. With a Virtual Office, adults with ADHD and others who have suffered from strokes or brain disorders might be able to retrain their memories or improve their ability to do two or more tasks at the same time.

While interviewing Rizzo, I found myself wondering if a Virtual Office might also someday be available to help writers get better organized.

Several groups of scientists around the world are looking for additional applications of virtual reality. One recent study found that the technology could help ease the suffering of children undergoing painful medical procedures. Kids who experienced a pleasant virtual reality while getting

- **What adults might benefit medically from virtual reality technology?**

• **How can virtual reality help kids undergoing painful medical procedures?**

blood drawn or having healthy skin grafted onto severely burned areas appeared to feel less pain than those who simply watched a cartoon. In this case, distraction was a goal, not a problem.

As new applications arise and computer technology improves, it may get harder and harder to distinguish between the real and the virtual. Don't get confused, though. Letting fly those paper airplanes might be okay in a virtual classroom, but it could get you into real trouble in a real one.

After Reading:

• **Why does Skip Rizzo think that psychology needs virtual reality to "keep pace with modern society"? What would keep psychology behind the times?**

• **What makes virtual reality different from today's standard computer programs? How could you make virtual reality even more realistic?**

• **Do you think the Virtual Classroom would be more efficient than other tests to evaluate students' problems?**

• **Do you think that the Virtual Classroom would increase or reduce the number of kids who take medication for ADHD? Why?**

A New Way to Read?

Do you like to read? If you're like some readers, you may collect so many books that they overflow your shelves and seem to be taking over your entire room. What if there were a way to read as many books as you wanted without ever adding to your bookshelf, if a single tiny computer could store all the books you've ever dreamed of reading? Computer scientists are actively working to make that dream a reality. As the next article shows, electronic paper may well be the wave of the future.

—The Editor

Roll-up Computer Monitors to Go

by Sorcha McDonagh

Have you noticed how gadgets are getting smaller? Cell phones, laptops, MP3 players—they're all getting slimmer and lighter.

Now, researchers at the companies Philips and E Ink have taken another step toward greater convenience. It's a new type of electronic paper that displays words and pictures, just like your computer monitor (Figure 1.2). But it's as thin as a sheet of regular paper. You can roll it up, fold it, or bend it. If you drop it, don't worry. It won't break.

The electronic paper has two main layers. The top layer is a plastic film that has tiny bubbles containing two types of ink, black and white. The bottom layer contains a network of tiny electronic circuits. These circuits are made out of a special type of plastic that conducts electricity.

How do these two layers work together to display a picture or words? First, the black and white inks have opposite electrical charges. When a particular voltage is applied to a bubble, the white ink rises to the top and the black ink sinks to the bottom, where you can't see it. And if a different voltage is applied, the opposite happens. The black ink rises while the white ink lays low.

Applying different voltages by way of the circuitry below the ink layer organizes the ink into various patterns, such as words and pictures. By switching the voltage pattern, the electronic-paper display can change a few times per second.

The scientists who developed the electronic paper claim that their version is the thinnest, most flexible yet. Previous versions of electronic paper were made with a thin sheet of glass, which was fragile and rigid.

Bas Van Rens at Philips in the Netherlands says that, within a couple of years, you could be using electronic

Figure 1.2 Electronic paper would allow you to read as many books or other documents as you wanted, or to have portable e-mail in a form much lighter and more convenient than a laptop computer.

paper to check your e-mail or to surf the Internet. When you're finished, you'd roll up your sheet of e-paper and tuck it away in your back pocket.

Going Deeper:

Goho, Alexandra. "Flexible E-paper: Plastic Circuits Drive Paperlike Displays." *Science News* 165(January 31, 2004): 67. Available online at *http://www.sciencenews.org/20040131/fob1.asp*.

You can learn more about electronic paper and ink online at *http://computer.howstuffworks.com/ e-ink.htm* and *www.media.mit.edu/micromedia/ elecpaper.html*.

Section 2

Robotics

When you hear the word *robot*, what comes to mind? If you're like most people, you probably envision a human-like figure made out of metal that can roll around independently and handle all kinds of chores without ever getting tired. In reality, most robots are nothing like the humanoid contraptions we see on television, but they are no less impressive.

Some of the robots on the cutting edge of technology today are built from automobiles and designed to cross over even the roughest terrain without the guidance of a human driver. You'll read about these robots in the first article of this section, about the Grand Challenge Race sponsored by the U.S. Defense Advanced Research Projects Agency (DARPA). Other robots, called "musclebots," are tiny devices that can be implanted in living tissue for various purposes, from delivering medication to making fine movements, as you'll learn in the second article.

Perhaps some of the most advanced robots in use today are the rovers that are now exploring the surface of the planet Mars, as part of a project for the National Aeronautics and Space Administration (NASA). These amazing vehicles can not only function efficiently and independently on the surface of an alien planet, but can take highly accurate measurements, photographs, and samples of soil and atmosphere to help scientists here on Earth learn more about outer space.

For now, robots may not be acting as servants in our private homes, but they are nonetheless making valuable contributions to our lives.

—The Editor

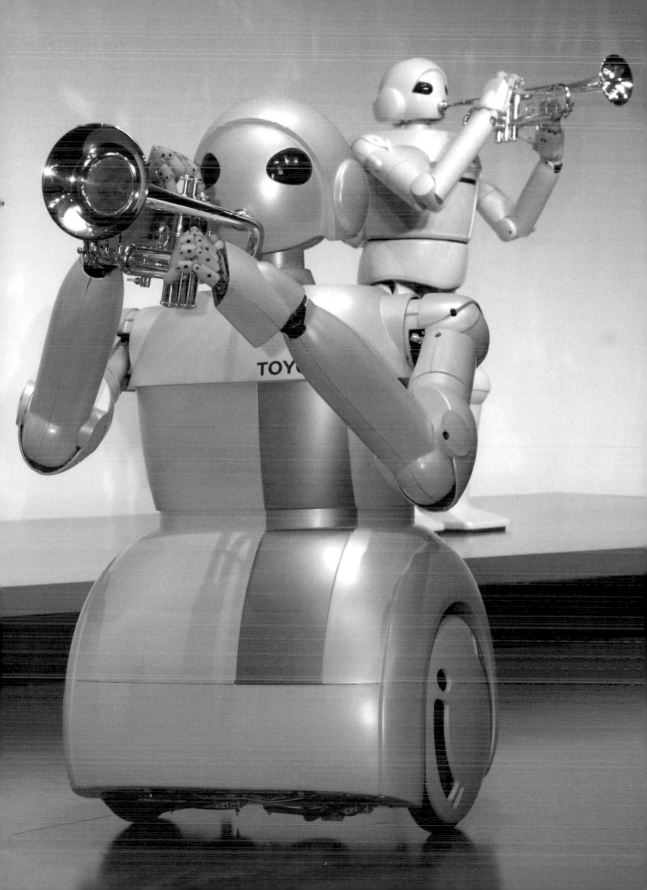

The Grand Challenge

Each year, the U.S. Defense Advanced Research Projects Agency (DARPA) sponsors a unique competition. It is a challenge to build a robotic vehicle. In the 2004 race, the goal was to create a robot that would be able to drive itself across the desert between Los Angeles, California, and Las Vegas, Nevada—a long distance over some of the harshest desert in the world. Why would a government agency want to develop self-navigating vehicles? Think about how much safer soldiers would be if robots could go into the heat of battle instead of human beings. The following article looks at the 2004 Grand Challenge, as DARPA's race is called, highlighting the successes and failures of the robot contestants and the possibilities for robotic vehicles in the future.

—The Editor

Robots on a Rocky Road

by Emily Sohn

> **Before Reading:**
>
> - **How far do you think an unmanned car equipped with sensors and navigation equipment could go on its own without crashing? What factors might determine the distance that the vehicle travels?**
>
> - **What is a "smart" technology?**

Here's the challenge. Design a vehicle that can travel 142 miles [229 km] across the desert between Los Angeles and Las Vegas. Your invention will have to stop at a number of checkpoints along the way, and it'll be racing more than a dozen other vehicles.

Here's the catch. Once it leaves the starting line, your vehicle has to drive itself.

Welcome to a recent competition sponsored by the U.S. Defense Advanced Research Projects Agency (DARPA). DARPA's Grand Challenge, held for the first time in March 2004, offered $1 million to the team whose vehicle completed the course in the shortest time.

> - **What does DARPA stand for?**

A wide variety of teams accepted the challenge, from high school students with a budget of just a few thousand dollars to professional engineers who had millions of dollars to burn. The contending vehicles included motorcycles, golf carts, sport utility vehicles, and a hybrid car with a gas-electric engine, all loaded up with computers and complicated gadgetry.

Among the 15 teams that made it to the final round on March 13, 2004, spirits were high when the race started at 6:30 A.M. in Barstow, California. Less than four hours later, all the vehicles had crashed, stalled, caught fire, or

Robot Racers on Venus

The U.S. Department of Defense sponsors a contest in which teams build vehicles that can drive themselves. To win in 2004, a vehicle had to be the first one to complete a 142-mile [229-km] course across rough desert terrain.

The teams selected a variety of names for their "smart" vehicles, including Sandstorm, Doom Buggy, Golem, CajunBot, Terrahawk, Auto Quad, Ghost Rider, Ladibug, and CyberRider.

Suppose that you are now building an autonomous vehicle that would be able to race across the surface of the planet Venus. Given the much more extreme conditions on Venus, in what ways would such a vehicle differ from one that could navigate a desert course on Earth? What name would you give it?

leaked oil. The vehicle that made it the farthest, from Carnegie Mellon University (CMU) in Pittsburgh, covered just 7.4 miles [12 km] before slamming into a roadside barrier that stopped it dead.

Based on these results, you might think that the competition was a total failure. After all, none of the machines even came close to finishing. To most team members and DARPA organizers, however, the first annual Grand Challenge was a great success.

"We were very, very satisfied with the performance of all the teams," said DARPA's Jan Walker. "We gave them a big challenge, and they really stepped up to it."

SMART MACHINES

No one really expected perfection on the first try.

According to DARPA, one main goal of the Grand Challenge is to push forward the technology for self-navigating, or autonomous, vehicles. Developing such vehicles will take time, and DARPA is trying to steer research in that direction.

"Smart" vehicles could replace people in battle and other dangerous situations, said Air Force Colonel Jose Negron, Grand Challenge program manager. He answered questions on the radio program *Science Friday* the day before the 2004 competition.

"The most important thing," Negron said, "is that this

technology will come back to the United States military to help save human lives."

The U.S. Congress has ordered the army to replace at least one-third of its battlefield vehicles with autonomous versions by the year 2015.

The other main goal of the competition is to seek out new ideas and technologies from people not already working with the military.

Anyone and everyone—students, backyard enthusiasts, the nation's top scientists—was invited to take part. "We're really trying to find that new idea out there," Negron said.

> • Why are self-controlled, or autonomous, vehicles important to the U.S. military?

NEW IDEAS

Indeed, ideas came from all over the place, and strategies were as varied as the people who came up with them. The most sophisticated technologies came from teams with the biggest budgets. Carnegie Mellon, for one, spent $3.5 million and had major sponsors backing its effort. Teams with less money had to be more crafty.

Still, vehicles in the competition shared some basic capabilities. For one thing, all had sensors that took in information about the world around them.

The Carnegie Mellon vehicle, a souped-up Humvee (HMMWV) called Sandstorm, had two cameras set up like a pair of eyes to produce three-dimensional images of the terrain in front of it. It also used radar and laser ranging to gather information about the vehicle's surroundings.

As data came pouring in from the sensors, on-board computers translated the information into a streaming view of the world. The vehicle then had to react appropriately, steering clear of boulders and other obstacles or staying on a steep, narrow, winding road.

In this year's Grand Challenge, DARPA officials didn't reveal the precise route until 4:00 A.M. of the day of the race. Teams then had just a few hours to load landmarks and other details into their vehicle computers and program **Global Positioning System** (**GPS**) receivers for navigation.

The route was a challenge for everybody. The first 5 miles [8 km] alone featured dirt roads, huge boulders, and lots of steep switchbacks.

- **Describe Carnegie Mellon's vehicle. How much did it cost?**

NEXT YEAR

Most teams left the competition determined to come back with better systems and vehicles. "We will improve the stereo cameras, radar, and laser immediately," said CMU team leader William L. "Red" Whitaker. The team also wants to enhance the vehicle's planning of its course.

The team's military surplus Humvee proved to be tough and reliable, Whitaker said. Nonetheless, it hopes to upgrade its vehicle to a newer model for next year's challenge in 2005.

CMU's team is into speed as much as accuracy, Whitaker emphasized. Sandstorm travels as fast as 40 miles [64 km] per hour.

While university engineers such as Whitaker were applying decades of experience to the challenge, teenagers from California were learning some lessons of their own. About 40 kids from Palos Verdes High School worked on a donated Acura, which qualified for the race.

"We used a laser rangefinder and GPS," said Nathan Howard, a 17-year-old junior with the Palos Verdes team. "We didn't read any technical manuals. We just sort of worked things out in our heads and programmed them up and then tested them out in the car."

On race day, the team's vehicle missed a turn near the start and crashed into a barrier. Next year, the students plan to reorganize their team into small work groups and focus on fine-tuning the car's steering components. They'll also apply some of the things they learned this year about planning and taking projects one step at a time.

Nevertheless, the students were happy with how they did. "I'm proud of our effort," Howard said. "It showed that our ideas were feasible and that the car could work."

Other teams were impressed, too.

"The most wonderful thing about this year's competition was meeting future generations that will do this kind of work," Whitaker said. "Kids out there should know that robotics is looking to them . . . to achieve what hasn't been done yet."

The next big idea could be yours. Start your engine!

> • **What happened to the Palos Verdes High School vehicle, Doom Buggy?**

After Reading:

- If you were to change the rules of the race, what would you suggest that DARPA do differently?

- Besides military applications, how else might "smart" cars benefit people?

- Name some other technologies that were originally designed for the military but are now used everyday by people who aren't in the military. (If you can't think of any examples, you can always do some research on the Internet.)

- Compare and contrast the advantages of using a vehicle such as a golf cart instead of a Humvee for the race.

- What were the main problems that prevented all of the vehicles from getting very far?

Robots With Muscles

Often, in science-fiction movies, we see "robots" that look and act just like real human beings. They have human-like bodies, including skin and muscles. Thanks to a recent invention, we may be well on the way to seeing these kinds of robots in real life. At the University of California, Los Angeles, scientists recently succeeded in creating "musclebots"—tiny robots built partly from the cells of animals (in this case, rats), that can move independently under the control of a computerized microprocessor. The following article by Emily Sohn examines this amazing development and explores the possible uses of this technology for the future of robotics.

—The Editor

Musclebots Take Some Steps

by Emily Sohn

You've probably heard of robots. Now, make way for musclebots.

Scientists in California have made tiny walking machines out of heart muscle grown from rat cells. When the muscle contracts, then relaxes, the musclebot takes a step. The entire device is tinier than a comma.

Viewed under a microscope, "they move very fast," says bioengineer Jianzhong Xi of the University of California, Los Angeles (UCLA). "The first time I saw that, it was kind of scary."

Scientists have already used muscle tissue to make machines, but these earlier machines were much larger than the new musclebots. A few years ago, for instance, a team at the Massachusetts Institute of Technology (MIT) made a palm-sized device, called a biomechatronic fish, which swam by using living muscle tissue taken from frogs' legs.

Adding muscles to a minuscule machine requires a different approach. Instead of using whole tissue, the scientists grew a thin film of heart muscle right on their bot. To do this, they borrowed some methods from the industry that makes chips for computers and other high-tech devices. But these methods can harm cells, so the team also invented some cell-friendly techniques to help do the job.

In the end, the musclebot looks like a golden arch, coated on its inner surface with muscle. Kept alive in a special solution containing **glucose**, the heart muscle cells beat, causing the bot to scoot along. When the muscle contracts, the arch squeezes together, and the back leg moves forward. When the muscle relaxes, the arch widens, and the front leg moves forward.

Researchers envision a number of applications for the new technology, including musclebots that deliver drugs directly to the cells that need them. They might also be useful for building other tiny machines, converting muscle motion into electric power for microcircuits, or studying muscle tissue.

So far, musclebots can move only in one direction, and they can't be easily turned on and off. Future versions are sure to be more versatile.

Going Deeper:

Weiss, Peter. "Micro Musclebot: Wee Walker Moves by Heart Cells' Beats." *Science News* 167(January 22, 2005): 53–54. Available online at *http://www.sciencenews.org/articles/20050122/fob6.asp*.

Robot Rovers

For centuries, people have wondered whether there might be intelligent life somewhere in outer space, beyond our home planet. Astronauts have traveled into space and even to the moon, but it is much more difficult to get to other planets. That's where robots come in. Not only can they handle the extreme conditions on alien planets like Mars, but they can also look for new forms of life in some of the harshest environments on Earth, such as the Atacama Desert of Chile. Scientists believe that if living things can survive in this kind of habitat, they may also exist in similar conditions in outer space. The following article explores the use of robots in the ongoing search for alien life.

—The Editor

Searching for Alien Life

by Emily Sohn

> **Before Reading:**
>
> • **What do you think "astrobiology" is?**
>
> • **Describe a desert.**
>
> • **What is a microhabitat?**

On a clear night, go outside, lie on your back, and stare into the sky. As you gaze at the multitude of stars, you might wonder: Is there life on other planets out there?

"That's one of the great questions of humanity," says David Wettergreen. He's a robotics scientist at Carnegie Mellon University in Pittsburgh.

"Are we alone or not?" Wettergreen asks. "You can spend your whole life pondering this question."

Instead of just thinking about the question, Wettergreen wants to answer it. And he's getting funds from the National Aeronautics and Space Administration (NASA) to help find an answer.

The space agency has a project called the Astrobiology Science and Technology Program for Exploring Planets (ASTEP). Astrobiology is the study of life in the universe. One way that NASA researchers have looked for signs of life in outer space is by sending signals into the void and listening for a response. So far, these messages have turned up nothing but silence.

Wettergreen has a different strategy, and it begins right here on Earth. In September 2004, he and his team traveled to one of the driest, most desolate places on the planet—the Atacama Desert in northern Chile. Conditions there are similar to conditions on Mars (Figure 2.1). And, because the landscape is so dry, scientists argue about whether any sort of life could possibly survive in the desert on its own.

In the Atacama, Wettergreen and a team of researchers use an equipment-loaded robot to search for pockets of life. The scientists want to learn if, how, and why anything can survive in such harsh conditions.

"Our ultimate goal is to discover something unique about the Atacama," says Wettergreen. In a broader sense, he says, the techniques used on the mission could eventually help astrobiologists explore other parts of the solar system.

"We're trying to learn about the desert," Wettergreen says, "and about how you go looking for life."

- **Why did Wettergreen and his colleagues travel to the Atacama Desert In Chile?**

ROVING ROBOT

The team's most valuable member is

not a person. It's a robot named Zoë. *Zoe* happens to be the Greek word for "life."

Zoë is about the size of an office desk (Figure 2.2). It's 1 meter [3.3 ft] high and 2 meters [6.6 ft] wide, and it weighs about 180 kilograms [397 lbs]. Its top speed is 1.2 meters [3.9 ft] per second. It carries an array of solar cells on its back to collect energy from the sun.

The robot is similar to the rovers *Spirit* and *Opportunity*, which are currently on Mars. The scientists give Zoë a general program telling it what to do. The

Figure 2.1 The terrain of the Atacama Desert closely resembles the harsh features on the surface of Mars, seen here.

vehicle then explores the landscape. As it cruises around, Zoë sends data back to the researchers. Nobody drives it, and there's no remote control.

• **Describe Zoë's cameras.**

Using a robot allows the researchers to take frequent measurements over a large area, creating a sort of catalog of what's out there.

In 2003, the team spent about a month in the Atacama just developing and testing instruments for Zoë. The robot carries three sophisticated cameras that record everything in very clear, color images. To mimic the three-dimensional view that a person would have while walking around, the cameras sit close to each other just above eye-level.

To detect microscopic life on the ground, Zoë carries a fluorescence imager.

Fluorescence occurs when a substance absorbs certain kinds of electromagnetic radiation, such as ultraviolet light or X-rays, and gives off visible light of a particular color in return. As soon as the ultraviolet light or other source is turned off, the substance stops giving off visible light.

Because different materials absorb and give off different colors of light, Zoë can detect and distinguish between various kinds of minerals and molecules.

Zoë also carries a **spectrometer**, which analyzes

• **How does Zoë distinguish between different minerals and molecules?**

how objects in the soil reflect light. The spectrometer detects which particular colors, or wavelengths, of visible and infrared light are reflected by soil particles. Like fingerprints, particular patterns of wavelengths correspond to different minerals.

The robot also has a plow that can turn over rocks and dig into the soil, allowing the fluorescence imager and spectrometer to examine what's under the surface.

FIELD LIFE

Even though the robot does much of the work during the research mission, life in the field isn't easy for the researchers. "We work from dawn until dusk, seven days a week," Wettergreen says. The scientists and technicians have to make sure that Zoë is working correctly, and they must sift through loads of data transmitted by the robot.

The environment can be hard to adjust to. Less than a centimeter of rain falls on the Atacama every year. A bone dry, rocky landscape stretches as far as the eye can see. There are no trees, no lakes, no little animals scurrying around. The only contrast is the brilliantly blue, cloudless sky above.

"In the Atacama, you see rock and soil in all directions and really nothing else," Wettergreen says. "When you look up, it's blue. When you look down, it's brown. With the midday sun overhead beating down on you, it does seem desolate."

Still, Wettergreen and his colleagues are convinced that there is more to the Atacama than meets the eye, and they're determined to prove it.

"We are finding that the desert is not uniform," he says. "There are microhabitats, small oases. Sometimes a single rock provides shelter or a trap for moisture."

Figure 2.2 Zoë the robot is helping scientists in the search for life in outer space.

• **What are conditions like in the Atacama Desert?**

Water is often the first sign that there might be life around.

If Zoë finds good ways to look for these hidden specks of life, scientists might eventually make similar discoveries on Mars and beyond. That would answer one of life's biggest questions, and stargazing would gain a whole new meaning.

After Reading:

• **Why would scientists need to work with a robot like Zoë?**

• **To survive the harsh conditions of the Atacama Desert, what do you think the scientists need to bring along?**

• **Why has the team testing its robot in the Atacama Desert set up a Website?**

• **What kind of life is Zoë looking for?**

• **How does a microhabitat work? Besides the desert, where else might such habitats exist?**

• **Why might life found in a desert be similar to life on Mars?**

Section 3

Transportation

The quest to find better ways to get around is as old as human life itself. From the invention of the wheel to the age of automobiles to the era of space exploration, people have spent centuries working to improve transportation.

One of the most pressing issues in transportation is finding the best available fuel to propel vehicles without damaging the environment. The first articles in this section take a look at new fuel sources for automobiles and the use of solar sails—devices that catch the rays of the sun and use it to produce energy that can move a spacecraft.

Although flying is already the fastest way for us to get from one place to another, scientists are always hoping to make flight even faster. Sorcha McDonagh's article "Flying the Hyper Skies" examines the Hyper-X, an experimental aircraft that is being tested to see whether flying faster than the speed of sound can be done regularly and efficiently. The fourth article looks at the use of remote-controlled aircraft to see what impact they may have on the future of transportation.

Despite the fact that scientists and engineers have been working for many years to improve the ways we travel, the basic design of most vehicles—cars, airplanes, and boats—hasn't changed much over time. In her article "Are Propellers Fin-ished?", author Carrie Lock takes a look at ongoing research into methods of changing the way boats move through water, inspired by observations of how animals like whales and birds use their bodies to move quickly.

—The Editor

Environmentally Friendly Cars

The invention of the automobile dramatically changed the way people live. Instead of having to live in the cities to be near their jobs, people could now live in the less-crowded suburbs and commute to work each day. Cars also made it easier for people to travel and to stay in touch with friends and family. Unfortunately, these positive changes came at a price—severe damage to the environment from the pollution caused by burning fuel. Today, scientists are trying to find ways to keep the convenience of cars but get rid of the pollution they create. In this article, Emily Sohn takes a look at some of the latest innovations in environmentally friendly vehicles, from hybrid cars to the use of hydrogen instead of oil for fuel.

—The Editor

Revving Up Green Machines

by Emily Sohn

People love their "zoom, zoom." In the United States alone, 17 million new cars hit the road in 2004.

But the freedom to travel anywhere, anytime in a car or truck comes at a price. And it's not just the cost of gasoline, insurance, and repairs. Automobiles are a major source of pollution. Most cars burn gasoline, which releases carbon dioxide gas into the air, along with other particles and pollutants.

To help counter soaring gas prices and reduce air pollution, researchers are looking into new ways to make cars run more efficiently with less impact on the environment.

Some environmentally friendly "green" cars already on the street use a mixture of gas and electricity. When such a **hybrid** vehicle stops, its gas engine shuts down and an electric motor powered by batteries takes over. When the car speeds up, the engine starts, moving the car and recharging the batteries. At high speeds, the gas engine and electric motor operate together.

More futuristic technologies involve the use of hydrogen as a fuel. Some companies have already built vehicles that run on hydrogen, but many obstacles remain before you'll see a lot of hydrogen-powered cars on the road and hydrogen filling stations where you can refuel.

HYDROGEN POWER

Getting energy out of hydrogen to power a car involves a device called a fuel cell.

A molecule of hydrogen consists of two hydrogen atoms. In a typical fuel cell, a metal such as platinum splits up hydrogen molecules. The process releases electrons, which generate an electric current that can be used to run a motor. The hydrogen atoms, which have each lost an electron, combine with oxygen from the air in another part of the fuel cell. When two hydrogen atoms combine with one oxygen atom, the result is a molecule of water (H_2O).

So, the only "waste" product is water. That's pretty clean!

Hydrogen is an appealing carrier of energy, says Nathan Glasgow. He's a consultant at the Rocky Mountain Institute in Snowmass, Colorado. The element is light, stable, and highly abundant, he says.

Getting a good supply of hydrogen, however, is harder than you might think. The problem is that most hydrogen on Earth is attached to something else, mainly carbon or oxygen.

It takes a lot of energy to break apart water and other

molecules to get the hydrogen out. This energy usually comes from burning oil or coal, which produces lots of carbon dioxide and other pollutants.

It might be better, for example, to use wind power instead of coal or oil to provide the energy to split water. However, the windiest places, such as North Dakota, are far from where most people live. So, the hydrogen would need to be stored and shipped.

Right now, there's no system of pipes for transporting hydrogen. And that's a major problem, Glasgow says. "We have to find a way to move it around."

RUN TIMES

Another challenge is getting enough juice from hydrogen to keep a car running for a long time. Right now, a tank of hydrogen can propel a car only about 100 or 150 miles [161 or 241 km]. That means refueling a lot more often than most people would like.

Today's fuel cells are also expensive. A fuel-cell-powered car might cost more than 10 times as much as a gas-powered car would cost.

And fuel cells wear out faster than gas engines. Typical fuel cells for cars have an operating lifetime of about 1,000 hours of driving time. A gas engine lasts at least 5,000 hours, spread over more than 10 years.

Nonetheless, the U.S. government has pledged more

than $1 billion toward the effort to improve hydrogen fuel cell technology. Three states—California, Florida, and New York—plan to spend millions in the next five years to test electric cars powered by hydrogen and build a network of hydrogen filling stations. A hydrogen pump opened in 2005 in Washington, D.C.

There's a long way to go. "We don't think mobile fuel cells are going to come on-line for another 20 years," Glasgow says.

NEW MATERIALS

In the meantime, scientists and environmentalists are pushing other strategies for making cars that are less harmful to the environment. The Rocky Mountain Institute, for instance, supports a move toward lighter automobiles.

The lighter a car, Glasgow says, the less energy (and fuel) that it takes to move it.

Think about how much harder it is to walk up stairs with a heavy load. "If your backpack itself weighs 50 pounds [23 kg], and then you start putting books in, it doesn't make any sense," Glasgow says.

Heavy cars are just as inefficient. "You want to move people and cargo," he says. "There's no value added in moving a large, heavy car, too."

To make cars lighter and cheaper while keeping their

size and strength, Glasgow says, companies are trying out new materials. Extra-light steel, ceramics, aluminum with titanium or magnesium, and other materials borrowed from the aerospace industry are a few examples.

One company is now putting lightweight carbon fibers into some of its cars' roofs and hoods to lighten the load.

Making automobiles lighter would also be a huge step toward making fuel cells practical when they become cheaper and more readily available, Glasgow says.

FUTURE TRAVEL

For now, hybrid cars that save fuel by running partly on electricity are becoming increasingly popular. So is the use of alternative fuels, such as natural gas and biodiesel, which can come from vegetable oil, animal fat, or recycled restaurant grease.

There might be even more options available by the time you get your learner's permit, if you haven't started driving already. And, in another generation or so, you could be zooming around in a hydrogen-fueled car.

Solar Sails

You've probably seen houses with solar panels for energy or small devices like calculators that run on the power of the sun. But you may not realize that the rays of the sun can be harnessed to provide energy for much, much larger machines—like spacecraft. In the next article, we learn about the solar sails scientists are working on to try to make solar-powered space travel a reality.

—The Editor

Riding Sunlight

by Emily Sohn

Before Reading:

- **Why would scientists want to use solar power to propel a spaceship?**

- **How is space travel like sailing a ship?**

Hundreds of years ago, sailing ships carried explorers across the ocean from Europe to America and beyond. A future generation of explorers might set sail, too—not across water, but across outer space.

In 2005, researchers planned to test a solar sail spacecraft that uses sunlight instead of wind to move.

In theory, spacecraft pushed by light could cruise at high speeds without using any fuel. Fast and practical travel to other planets and even stars might then become possible.

The first solar sail flight could be monumental, says Louis Friedman. It could have the same sort of impact as the pioneering airplane flight made by the Wright brothers in 1903.

Before the Wright brothers and other inventors showed the way, the idea of humans in flight seemed ridiculous to many people. A hundred years later, passenger jets and private planes crisscross the sky all day long.

Now, it's the idea that sunlight can propel spacecraft that many people find hard to believe. Friedman and others are trying to turn this crazy idea into reality.

The biggest challenge is figuring out how to do what you know should be possible, Friedman says. The forces are there. It's a matter of harnessing them. Friedman heads the *Cosmos 1* solar sail project. He's also executive director of The Planetary Society in Pasadena, California.

"The Wright brothers flew for 12 seconds," Friedman says. "They went nowhere, but they were successful. If we can fly for just 2 days, it'll be a success."

- **Why does Louis Friedman compare the flight of *Cosmos 1* to the Wright brothers' first flight?**

SOLAR PRESSURE

Sailing in space is similar to sailing on water, with two major differences. There's no water in space. And there's no wind.

This may sound confusing because there is something called a **solar wind**. Unlike the breezes we're used to on Earth, however, the solar wind is a stream of particles spit out by the sun. Magnetic fields help protect our planet from these particles.

Solar sailing has nothing to do with the solar wind. Instead, solar sails catch rays of light (Figure 3.1).

• What is solar wind?

It may be hard to imagine, but sunlight itself can make objects move. Light is a form of energy, and it exerts pressure.

We don't feel the pressure of sunlight on Earth because other forces that act on us are much stronger. Outer space, however, is practically empty. Nothing gets in the way of the force exerted by light.

Understanding how solar sails work also hinges on a law of physics discovered by Isaac Newton in the 1600s. His third law of motion states that for every action, there's an equal and opposite reaction.

For example, when you let air out of a balloon, the air shoots out in one direction and the balloon zips off in the opposite direction. On a skateboard, pushing your foot back makes the board go forward.

Solar sails have mirror-like blades that reflect sunlight. When light gets reflected back in one direction, the sail moves in the opposite direction.

• How is Newton's third law of motion involved in solar sailing?

LIGHT TRAVEL

Light exerts only a tiny amount of force. So, to get a real

push, a solar sail must be as large and lightweight as possible.

The solar sail developed by Friedman's team is made of a very light, shiny plastic. It has eight blades, arranged in a circle. Each blade is 15 meters (50 feet) long and even thinner than an ordinary garbage bag.

Figure 3.1 Solar sails like this one catch the rays of the sun and use it for power.

At first, a solar sail might travel at no more than a few millimeters a second—slower than a snail. With nothing in space to slow it down, though, the sail could, in theory, reach speeds as high as 100,000 miles [160,934 km] per hour, Friedman says. That would be fast enough to get to other planets in just a few years.

- **Why must the sails of a solar spacecraft be large and lightweight?**

Changing the angle of its sails would allow the spacecraft to change direction. It's like using a rudder to control a boat's direction.

- **How does a spacecraft driven by solar sails change direction?**

LAUNCH DATE

Friedman's team planned to launch its solar sail spacecraft, *Cosmos 1*, in March 2005. This would be the first attempt to get light pressure to propel a vehicle in outer space.

People are skeptical. "Even I'm not sure the first attempt will succeed," Friedman says. "But I don't think anyone thinks the theory is wrong."

Friedman imagines a day in the distant future when solar sails would crowd space in the same way that airplanes crowd the sky on Earth today. For now, he and his team would be happy to take even a small step toward an entirely new category of space exploration.

"We know with other inventions that people try, fail, try again, and then succeed," Friedman says.

The dramatic flight of *Cosmos 1* may turn out to be the start of a great adventure.

After Reading:

- **Why does solar sailing make sense in space but not on Earth?**

- **Does solar sailing make sense for transporting people to other planets? Why or why not?**

- **Find pictures of a jet airliner and a spaceship. In what ways are the designs of these vehicles different? In what ways are they similar?**

- **Design an experiment that illustrates Newton's third law of motion. For examples, see *www.spartechsoftware.com/reeko/ Experiments/ExpMilkCartonWheel.htm* (*Reeko's Mad Scientist Lab*) or *www.iit.edu/ ~smile/ph9408.html* (*Illinois Institute of Technology*).**

- **_Cosmos 1_ was scheduled to be launched from a submarine. In what other ways could the space- craft be put into Earth orbit?**

- **Space travel tends to be very expensive. Do you think using solar power would make it cheap- er? Why or why not?**

Going Supersonic

In October 1947, American pilot Chuck Yeager made history when he flew his plane faster than the speed of sound. Since his remarkable achievement, scientists have continued to look for ways to make airplanes travel faster and more safely. The next article examines the development of Hyper-X, an experimental aircraft that travels at **supersonic** speeds.

—The Editor

Flying the Hyper Skies

by Sorcha McDonagh

A little airplane has given new meaning to the term "going hyper."

The Hyper-X recently broke the record for air-breathing jet planes when it traveled at a **hypersonic** speed of seven times the speed of sound. That's about 5,000 miles [8,047 km] per hour. At this speed, you'd get around the world—flying along the equator—in less than five hours.

The Hyper-X is an unmanned, experimental aircraft just 12 feet [3.7 meters] long (Figure 3.2). It achieves hypersonic speed using a special sort of engine known as a **scramjet**. It may sound like something from a comic book, but engineers have been experimenting with scramjets since the 1960s.

For an engine to burn fuel and produce energy, it needs oxygen. A jet engine, like those on passenger airplanes, gets oxygen from the air. A rocket engine typically goes faster but has to carry its own supply of oxygen. A scramjet engine goes as fast as a rocket, but it doesn't have to carry its own oxygen supply.

A scramjet's special design allows it to extract oxygen from the air that flows through the engine. And it does so without letting the fast-moving air put out the combustion flames. However, a scramjet engine works properly only at speeds greater than five times the speed of sound.

A booster rocket carried the Hyper-X to an altitude of about 100,000 feet [30,480 meters] for its test flight. The aircraft's record-beating flight lasted just 11 seconds.

In the future, engineers predict, airplanes equipped with scramjet engines could transport cargo quickly and cheaply to the brink of space. Hypersonic airliners could carry passengers anywhere in the world in just a few hours.

Figure 3.2 NASA's Hyper-X is an experimental aircraft designed to fly at speeds seven times faster than the speed of sound.

Out of the three experimental Hyper-X aircraft built for NASA, only one is now left. The agency has plans for another, 11-second hypersonic flight, this time at 10 times the speed of sound.

Hang on tight!

Going Deeper:

Weiss, Peter. "Soaring at Hyperspeed: Long-sought Technology Finally Propels a Plane." *Science News* 165(April 3, 2004): 213–214. Available online at *http://www.sciencenews.org/articles/20040403/fob6.asp*.

You can learn more about NASA's Hyper-X plane online at *http://oea.larc.nasa.gov/PAIS/FS-2003- 07-77-LaRC.html* and *www.nasa.gov/missions/research/x43-main.html*.

The Future of Remote-Controlled Planes

It's been more than a century since human beings discovered how to fly, and during most of that time, almost
all flights have been done in airplanes operated by trained
pilots. What if a plane could fly accurately on its own,
without needing a living pilot on board? The possibilities
are endless, especially for defense missions and wartime
flying. In this article, Emily Sohn describes the successful
flight of a remote-controlled model plane across the vast
expanse of the Atlantic Ocean, and explores what this
feat may mean for the future of flight.

—The Editor

Model Plane Flies the Atlantic

by Emily Sohn

Before Reading:

- Have you ever seen or used a model airplane? If you have, describe the plane and where you saw it. What powered the model airplane?

- How many famous aviators and important pilots can you name? List their names and when they made their noteworthy flights.

When Maynard Hill decided he wanted to fly a model airplane across the Atlantic Ocean, no one took him seriously.

"To be perfectly honest, most of us thought he was crazy," says Dave Brown, president of the Academy of Model Aeronautics and an old friend of Hill's. "We didn't think it could be done."

Sometimes, daring to be crazy pays off. Last summer, one of Hill's creations became the first model airplane to cross the Atlantic.

Named TAM-5, the 11-pound [5-kg] plane flew 1,888 miles [3,038 km] from Canada to Ireland in 38 hours, 53 minutes. It set world records for longest distance and longest time ever flown by a model airplane.

The achievement came at a symbolic time in the history of flight. One hundred years before, on December 17, 1903, the Wright brothers made the first powered, sustained, and controlled flight in a heavier-than-air flying machine at Kitty Hawk, North Carolina. Their plane covered a grand distance of 120 feet [37 meters] in about 12 seconds.

TAM-5's route also had historical significance. The model airplane followed the same path as the first nonstop, manned flight across the Atlantic in 1919. And Amelia Earhart left from a nearby spot in Newfoundland when she became the first woman to cross the Atlantic in 1928.

AUGUST LAUNCH

Hill, who is 77, legally blind, and mostly deaf, began his project 10 years ago. With the help of a support team, he made his first three attempts in August 2002. He figured August would be the best time to launch because that's the month with fewest storms, and wind conditions are usually favorable.

- Where did Hill's plane take off from and land? Why did Hill's team pick these particular take-off and landing locations?

None of the planes flew more than 500 miles [805 km], less than one-third of the way to Ireland. "As we put it," Brown says, "we fed them to the Atlantic." The first plane the team sent up in the summer of 2003 flew about 700 miles [1,127 km] before plunging into the sea.

At about 8:00 P.M. on August 9, 2003, Hill went for attempt number five. He had traveled from his home in Silver Spring, Maryland, to Cape Spear, Newfoundland, to toss TAM-5 into the air. Once the plane was airborne, a pilot on the ground used a remote control to steer the plane until it reached a cruising altitude of 300 meters [984 feet]. Then, a computerized **autopilot** took over.

For the next day and a half, everyone on the crew held his or her breath. "We were very much on pins and needles," says Brown, who went to Ireland to land the plane.

They had plenty of reasons to feel nervous. To qualify for flight records, a model airplane has to weigh less than 11 pounds [5 kg], including fuel. So, TAM-5 had room to carry just under 3 quarts [2.8 liters] of gas. This meant that the plane had to get the equivalent of about 3,000 miles [4,828 km] per gallon of fuel, Brown says. By comparison, a commercial jet can burn more than 3 gallons [11 liters] of fuel every mile.

The biggest challenge in building the model, Brown says, was figuring out how to make TAM-5's engine efficient enough to cross the ocean. Most model airplanes use alcohol-based fuels. Instead, Hill used Coleman lantern fuel because, he says, it's more pure and performs better. He tweaked a regular model airplane engine to make the valves smaller and more efficient.

The plane also carried an impressive set of electronics. Every hour during the flight, crew members were able to get information about the plane's location from a Global Positioning

• According to Brown, what was the airplane's "biggest challenge?"

System (GPS) device on board. The GPS device communicated with a satellite orbiting Earth to determine the plane's exact **latitude**, **longitude**, and speed.

The route was programmed into the computerized autopilot, which automatically adjusted the plane's direction to stay on course. There was also a transmitter on board that sent signals directly to crewmembers on the ground when the plane was within 70 miles [113 km] of its launch and landing sites.

ROUGH SPOTS

Everything went smoothly until about 3:00 A.M. on the second day of flight. Then, suddenly, the GPS unit stopped sending information. Everyone assumed the worst—until data started pouring in again three hours later. The satellite had just been busy for a while.

Even then, the model's arrival was never a sure thing. TAM-5's flight plan was programmed to use 2.2 ounces [62 g] of fuel per hour.

• What is a GPS device, and how does it work?

Crew members estimated that burning fuel at this rate would give the plane between 36 and 37 hours of flying time. They counted on having a good tailwind to push the plane to a cruising speed of about 55 miles [89 km] per hour. When data came streaming back in at 6:00 A.M., though, the plane was moving at only 42 miles [68 km] per hour. Apparently, there was no wind at all.

TAM-5 had already been flying for more than 38 hours when it finally came into view in Ireland. Brown was sure it was running on fumes. "The whole crew had visions of seeing the thing appear on the horizon," Brown says, "then quit and fall in the ocean."

With a remote control, he took over the plane's flight in stages: first steering, then altitude. At a few minutes after 2:00 P.M. on August 11, TAM-5 landed safely just 88 meters [289 ft] from the chosen spot on Mannin Bay, Galway. Cheers went up among the crowd of 50 or so people who had gathered to watch it land. "It was absolutely euphoric to see it arrive," Brown says.

Brown's wife was on the phone with Hill in Canada at the time. His reaction was even more emotional. "When the plane landed in Ireland," Hill says, "I was so overjoyed I hugged my wife and cried."

NOTHING FANCY

Amidst the celebration, Brown took the model apart to

check how much fuel was left. He found just 1.8 ounces [51 g], almost nothing. Later, the team realized that the flight plan had been set to burn 2.01 ounces [57 g] of fuel per hour instead of 2.2 [62.4 g]. The plane had wobbled up and down as a result, but the mistake was probably the secret of its success.

While Brown was working, he overheard one boy say to another, "That model isn't very fancy." This was quite true. TAM-5 was made of balsa wood and fiberglass, and it was covered with a plastic film, just like any ordinary model airplane. At 74 inches [188 cm] long and with a 72-inch [183-cm] wingspan, it used the same principles of flight as any other airplane, model or life-sized. "Yeah," the other boy said. "I bet I could build one that good."

The conversation forced Brown to reflect on the importance of TAM-5's record-setting flight. "I realized later that the most important significance wasn't the accomplishment itself but what it will challenge someone else to do," he says. "Perhaps even that kid, or some adult down the road, will build one that's better, or one that goes higher, faster, farther. That kind of challenge is what setting records is all about."

For Hill, the accomplishment holds a lesson in persistence. Keep trying, no matter what kind of handicaps you have, he says.

- **What records did this plane's flight set?**

"Kids can learn that it's often necessary to try and try again to achieve a goal," Hill says. "Don't give up! I have worked on model airplane records for 40 years. This particular goal required 5 years of building and testing—and crashing!"

It's impossible to know what TAM-5's flight will lead to next. If a small model airplane can fly across the ocean, maybe someday jets will be able to carry cargo the same distance without a single human on board, Brown says.

Other consequences may emerge that nobody has dreamed of yet, Brown says. "When the Wright brothers finished their first flight," he says, "if you had asked them what this means for the future, I don't think they would have told you that some day a 747 would fly across the country. They wouldn't have foreseen a flight to the moon."

So, it's onward and upward!

After Reading:

- Although this story is about a model airplane, how might the information learned by these model enthusiasts benefit those in other professions?

- The GPS device was incredibly important to this flight. What would you have done if you could not use this machine?

- Why do you think that Hill's team built the plane out of fiberglass and balsa wood? How would the flight have been affected if they had built the plane out of metal?

- If you wanted to learn about making a more efficient engine—as Hill had to—what resources would you seek?

- What kinds of experts would you want on your team to help a model plane cross the Atlantic Ocean? Create a team of four experts and explain why you picked each person.

Animal Antics Inspire Transportation Design

The development of the many modes of transportation that are currently available was an incredible feat of engineering. As sophisticated as our vehicles may be, though, they just can't do the same things that people and animals can, especially in the water. A boat or submarine can't flip itself smoothly around in the water to adjust to changing currents. What if it could? Scientists are studying the way aquatic animals move in the hope of figuring out how to improve the design of the watercraft.

—The Editor

Are Propellers Fin-ished?

by Carrie Lock

> **Before Reading:**
>
> - **Name three animals that have flippers.**
>
> - **Why are submarines useful?**
>
> - **What is "aquabatics"?**

If you've ever been to an aquarium or a zoo, you've probably admired the feisty penguins. They can squiggle through water faster than 10 miles [16 km] per hour, turn on a dime, and leap onto shore, all in one smooth movement.

Dolphins and seals can perform similar aquabatics.

These marine animals are more than just fun to watch. They're also inspiring engineers to look for better ways of propelling boats. You never see a submarine do what a penguin can do, but wouldn't it be cool if it could?

Propellers let ships travel in a relatively straight line over great distances. Today's engineers are trying to design vessels that can do a lot more than that. They want boats able to withstand stormy conditions that would shatter an existing craft. They want boats that can maneuver quickly in tight spaces. They want boats that can sense currents or waves and respond in a split second to hold their position. In effect, they want to reinvent the penguin—or perhaps the whale or fish.

A penguin's flippers are a good starting point.

ALL DRESSED UP

Propeller blades just spin. Penguin flippers do much more.

A penguin's flipper is like a hard, stiff paddle covered with tiny feathers. It's shaped a bit like an airplane wing. A flipper can flap up and down, move forward and backward, and twist around at the joint where it's attached to the penguin's body.

At the Massachusetts Institute of Technology (MIT), researchers are working on a new propulsion system for ships that mimics a penguin's flippers. Their artificial wooden flippers move a boat forward or backward by generating high-energy rings of spinning water. Other flipper movements steer the craft right, left, up, or down.

The MIT team is now testing how various flipper movements affect a boat's motion, doing experiments in giant basins of water.

The scientists envision using a pair of flippers in place of a propeller to move a boat along. More futuristic vessels could have as many as 50 flapping flippers, each one moving independently.

But it'll take many more years of research before the Navy or anyone else can launch high-tech ships driven by flippers.

A NEW KIND OF FIN

Flexibility also helps move things along in water.

> • Why are scientists looking at penguins to improve submarines?

Marine animals such as dolphins and seals aren't made of stiff materials. They're squishy, like human skin and muscle.

Flexible materials can store energy in ways that stiff ones can't. When a dolphin flexes its tail as far as it'll bend, it stores energy in its body—just like a stretched rubber band. When the tail slams down and straightens, this stored energy is released, and the dolphin shoots forward.

Engineers at Nekton Research, a company in Durham, North Carolina, have designed flexible fins for an underwater vehicle to take advantage of such cycles of storing and releasing energy.

The craft, called PilotFish, is shaped like a giant egg with four fins coming out of its waist. It's more than 3 feet [1 meter] long and weighs 350 pounds [159 kg].

PilotFish can't travel long distances quickly. Instead, maneuverability is its specialty. And it can get

> • What is the advantage of flexible materials for water vehicles?

going in a fraction of a second. Moreover, unlike any other watercraft, it can stop almost instantaneously just by slamming its fins forward.

"The thing looks like it hit a wall. It stops dead," says Chuck Pell, who helped design the fins. "The only other things that can do that are alive."

PilotFish is designed to operate in water too turbulent for other craft. For example, it could be used to inspect the underwater portions of structures such as bridges and docks.

- **Describe PilotFish.**

A river's waves or current can easily overcome or carry away a propeller-driven craft before it can perform an inspection. In contrast, PilotFish reacts to its environment quickly enough to stay in place. If the craft encounters an unexpected object, it can immediately stop to avoid bumping into it. If a wave rolls it over, PilotFish can right itself before the next wave comes.

To accomplish all this, PilotFish's fins generate huge forces. "You have to careful around it. You could break an arm," Pell says. He notes that he once ended up with a sprained wrist when a moving fin accidentally struck his hand.

WHALE WATCH

For their size, humpback whales are surprisingly agile.

This 50-foot [15-meter], 30-ton [27 metric-ton] animal can swim in a tight corkscrew pattern, sometimes less than 10 feet [3 meters] across.

• **Explain the effect of turbulent water on most underwater vehicles. Why is the PilotFish different?**

The whales do this not for fun but to capture a meal. They blow bubbles as they swim in this spiral pattern, creating a rising barrier around a cylinder of water. Tiny shrimp and small fish get trapped in the cylinder, and the whale simply swims up through the concentrated feast for its meal.

Scientists have long wondered how humpbacks manage this feat. They've been particularly curious about bumps along the leading edge of a humpback's long, narrow flippers.

To find out, researchers built two artificial whale flippers. One flipper had a scalloped edge, and the other was smooth. They then tested the two flippers in a wind tunnel. Although air is much less dense than water, it's still a fluid, and the researchers could adjust the air's speed so that it behaved like water rushing over a humpback's flipper.

The scientists found that the bumps reduce **drag** and increase a flipper's lift so it behaves more like an airplane wing. This extra lift and reduced drag lets a humpback whale make sharper turns than other whales can make.

Someday, engineers designing flippers or fins to drive boats and submarines might add bumps or scallops, too.

KAYAK FLIPPERS

Artificial fins inspired by one marine animal, the penguin, are already available—though not where scientists might have predicted. They're in a foot-powered propulsion system for kayaks designed by engineers at Hobie Cat in Oceanside, California.

> • How are scientists researching the role of a whale flipper's scalloped edge?

Instead of paddling, you sit in the kayak and pedal with your feet. Your pedaling powers two flexible fins.

At the start of each stroke, the fins twist and flex in such a way that they assume the shape of a propeller blade. A penguin's flipper flexes in the same way when the swimming bird wants to move itself forward.

The fins move larger volumes of water than a traditional oar can yet require less energy to do so. This lets kayakers go farther and faster, without getting as tired as when paddling with oars.

> • What is the advantage of pedaling rather than rowing a kayak?

Hobie Cat's pedaled kayaks are leading the way in applications of nature-inspired flipper design. Other applications are bound to follow.

Maybe someday you'll be able to

go to an aquarium show featuring underwater vehicles, gliding gracefully, racing around rocks, and leaping out of the water to wow a crowd—doing what comes naturally to penguins and dolphins.

After Reading:

- What other animals might it be useful for engineers to study in the search to improve transportation? Why?

- Why is it important for people to be able to look at the underwater parts of bridges?

- Think of a commercial use not mentioned in this article for a new, more agile water vehicle. Why would people want to buy such a watercraft?

- How might underwater vehicles need to be different for different locations? For example, why wouldn't a boat able to travel on a crowded river with lots of other boats be suitable for traveling along a rocky, stormy seacoast?

- Go to a local aquarium or zoo and pick an aquatic animal. Spend at least five minutes watching it. Describe its motions as carefully as you can. Include a drawing, if you wish.

- Compare the difficulties of designing an ideal vehicle for water with the difficulties of designing an ideal vehicle for land. What different problems must each vehicle overcome?

Section 4

Innovations

The whole point of new technology is to make life more convenient, healthier, and worthwhile, through improved communications, better transportation, or other innovations. The articles in this section examine some of the latest scientific research in fields that could have a profound impact on the way we live.

The first article explores the exciting innovation of using microchips in medicine. For centuries, doctors have prescribed medications to help cure or treat a wide array of ailments. But oral and even injectable medications have limitations. Only a single dose can be given at one time, which means that the patient has to keep taking the drug or getting injections to ease symptoms. The new technology described in the article uses tiny microchips, implanted in the body, to deliver measured doses of medication over a scheduled period of time, which means you wouldn't need to remember to take a pill every day. This kind of drug-delivery system could dramatically improve the lives of people with chronic illnesses that force them to spend hours counting out pills and setting medication schedules.

Scientists are also looking to nature to find ways to improve human-made items. By studying the materials animals and plants are made of, people are finding better methods of producing some of the things we use every day—from glue to dye to building bricks. Author Emily Sohn shows how copying nature—like the strong conch shell picture opposite—can help make even the most "unnatural" items much better.

Finally, we look a new ways to generate fuel that can be used to power planes, cars, and factories without damaging the environment.

—The Editor

Medical Microchips

If you suffer from allergies or some other chronic medical problem, you may have experienced the inconvenience of having to remember to take your medication at specific times of the day. Not only is it easy to forget your medicine, but swallowing lots of pills can be downright unpleasant. Just imagine what it must be like for people who have serious illnesses that require them to take lots of pills or get injections every single day of their lives. To try to make it easier for us to get the medicines we need, scientists are working to produce tiny chips that could be placed in the body and release the right dose of medication at the exact time we need it.

—The Editor

A Micro-dose of Your Own Medicine

by Sorcha McDonagh

"I promise, this won't hurt a bit," the doctor says, smiling. Then: jab. You've just gotten another shot.

If getting an injection isn't your idea of a good time, there's some promising news. Scientists have developed an amazing little device that could replace some injections—and pills, too.

The new device is a microchip that can be implanted in your body. The chip is about the size of a dime and is as thin as a piece of paper. On its surface are several small, sealed pockets for storing drug doses. These doses can be released into your body one by one at different times.

Each pocket is sealed with a different type of **polymer**, a material that has very long molecules. (Some of the natural substances in your body, such as proteins, are made of polymers.) By varying the length of the polymer molecules in the seals, the scientists can control when the drugs in each little pocket are released. Seals with longer polymer molecules take longer to break. Seals made with shorter polymer molecules will be the first to break and release drugs into your body.

With an implanted chip, you wouldn't need to

remember to take your medicine because the chip releases the drugs into your body for you, on schedule. The chip would also work well for certain types of **vaccines** that require several doses. Instead of making lots of trips to the doctor—and getting lots of injections—you'd only need to go once to have the chip implanted, and then the chip would take care of the rest.

So far, Robert Langer and his team at the Massachusetts Institute of Technology have made chips that can deliver drug doses for nearly five months. And after a chip has dispensed all of its medicine, it dissolves slowly inside your body.

This sort of chip isn't available to doctors yet, but when companies start making it, your doctor will then be able to say, "This really won't hurt a bit!"

Going Deeper:

Goho, Alexandra. "Timing Is Everything: Implantable Polymer Chip Delivers Meds on Schedule." *Science News* 164(October 25, 2003): 260. Available online at *http://www.sciencenews.org/20031025/fob3.asp*.

You can learn more about polymers online at *www.psrc.usm.edu/macrog/kidsmac/*.

Using Nature's Designs for the Products of Science

Plants and animals may not be as smart as we are, but in some ways, they have advantages that we don't. Different kinds of animals can perform amazing feats that we could never dream of—like walking on water and flying for hours or even days without getting tired. Imagine the possibilities if we could take a cue from nature and put some of the greatest natural materials and structural designs to work. That's just what some scientists are doing, as Emily Sohn shows us in the following article.

—The Editor

Inspired by Nature

by Emily Sohn

Before Reading:

- **Birds can fly. A water strider can walk on water. What ability that a plant or an animal has would you like to have yourself? Why?**

- **Why would scientists look to nature to improve technology or invent things?**

People do a lot of things that plants and animals can't do. We can talk and read. We can play computer games and go snowboarding—stuff that no worm or fern could ever do.

But nature is no slouch. There are lots of things that people wish they could do, and, in many cases, nature has already come up with a solution.

Some insects walk on water. Geckos can crawl across ceilings. Leaves turn sunlight into stored energy. Burrs stick to your socks like Velcro®. Certain birds sail on the wind for days without making any effort at all.

Often, millions of years of evolution have created the most efficient and environmentally friendly ways to do things, says author and environmentalist Janine Benyus.

Simple creatures, she says, "may harbor techniques that are in fact far more advanced than ours, and we can learn a lot from them."

Increasingly, scientists are catching on. Around the world, researchers are looking to nature for solutions to all sorts of problems. Inspired by nature, they're concocting stickier glues, stronger materials, zippier propellers, and much more.

The science of copying nature has come to be known as *biomimicry*, a word popularized by Benyus in a 1997 book with the same name.

The key is to ask yourself some basic questions about the world around you, Benyus says. What would nature do? And if it hasn't been done, why not?

- **What is bio-mimicry? Give two examples.**

STURDY SHELLS

What makes a material tough?

The giant pink queen conch, for instance, has a beautiful shell that's extremely strong and hard to break. This mollusk's shell is made almost entirely of a chalky mineral known as aragonite —a form of calcium carbonate. Yet the conch shell is hundreds of times stronger than the mineral by itself.

It turns out that the shell owes it strength to a secret ingredient—molecules known as **proteins**. These proteins form a kind of web that surrounds the mineral crystals and holds them together.

When you bang on a conch shell, it doesn't split. Instead, the shell develops tiny cracks that spread the impact throughout the material. This keeps the shell from breaking.

The scientists at Case Western Reserve University in Cleveland who made this discovery a few years ago and other researchers hope to use this information in their laboratories to make lightweight materials that are just as difficult to smash.

• **Why are conch shells tough to break?**

SNAGGING CARBON

When you breathe, you inhale oxygen and exhale carbon dioxide. A molecule of carbon dioxide is made up of one atom of carbon and two atoms of oxygen.

Plants have an amazing ability to remove carbon dioxide molecules from air, extract carbon atoms, and use them to make useful compounds, such as sugars.

At Cornell University, chemist Geoffrey Coates wants to make plastics the way nature's plants make sugars. His goal is to find materials that extract carbon directly from carbon dioxide as efficiently as plants do.

In another project inspired by nature, Coates recently discovered a way to make certain useful plastics from molecules found in many types of bacteria. Such plastics have the advantage of being **biodegradable**.

STICKY STUFF

Sometimes, it's useful to have materials stick together. That's where gecko tape might come in handy.

In 2003, scientists from Lewis & Clark College in Portland, Oregon, discovered how the hairs on a gecko's feet allow it to stick firmly to ceilings and even walk around on them.

Such information could lead to manufactured gecko tape. Imagine robots that can climb walls, ouch-less Band-Aids®, furniture padding that can easily be changed, and maybe even Spider-Man® gloves.

• **What uses could come out of the invention of "gecko tape"?**

Then there's color.

Blue jeans. Green hair. Purple plates. People often use dyes or **pigments** to color foods, fabrics, and lots of other materials. But many of these coloring agents are toxic. Using them can be messy and dangerous.

Nature has another answer. The brilliant blue of certain butterfly wings, for example, doesn't come from chemical pigments. Instead, the color comes from the way light is reflected by scales that cover the butterfly's wings. Such reflections also produce the iridescent colors of a peacock's feathers or the bright blue of a bluebird's plumage.

Some companies have started to use a similar strategy, creating patterns on surfaces to reflect certain colors of light, to make brilliantly colored objects or even new types of computer displays.

> • What problems exist with many dyes? How might biomimicry provide a way to help solve these problems?

HELPING BUILDERS

Biomimicry can help architects and builders design homes and other structures that improve people's lives, Benyus says.

To put up a sturdy building, for example, a construction company could pound steel columns deep into the ground to create a firm foundation. Or, a builder could try to copy the root systems of ancient trees that have kept enormous trunks upright for thousands of years.

Here's another example. Some desert-dwelling beetles have bumps on their stiff outer wings. The top of each bump is smooth, like glass, and attracts water. The troughs in between the bumps are covered with wax. Wax repels water.

On foggy mornings, tiny water droplets collect on the wings. The captured water droplets coalesce and grow, then roll off the backs of the beetles into their mouths.

Now, British engineers are making sheets and tiles with beetle-like bumps. Such a surface is covered with large numbers of tiny glass spheres, each about the size of a poppy seed, embedded in a thin layer of wax. Tents covered with this material could provide water for refugee camps and poor agricultural communities in drought-ridden nations.

Simple **mollusks**, such as mussels, can provide solutions for tricky household and even industrial problems.

Benyus once went to the Galapagos Islands in the Pacific Ocean with a group of wastewater treatment engineers. One problem the group faced was stopping the mineral buildup and scaling that often clogs or ruins pipes.

For an answer, they looked to the way mollusks make shells. The shells of these animals are basically built out of the same minerals that can clog pipes --calcium carbonate. Because the shells grow to a certain size and no larger, these animals have a way to stop the buildup of minerals. They release a special protein to do so.

One company has used these proteins as a model to create a line of products for preventing **corrosion**. The company describes their corrosion-preventing proteins as "nonhazardous, nontoxic, hypoallergenic, environmentally friendly, and biodegradable."

Other companies are looking to plants that naturally

resist toxic mold and repel dangerous microbes to inspire coatings for walls in houses. The lotus plant is famous for making water bead up and roll right off. Now, it's possible to build lotus-like walls that don't need to be scrubbed. Rainwater by itself cleans them off.

NATURE BY DESIGN

The ultimate goal, Benyus says, is to mimic not just materials but entire processes in nature.

For example, instead of cutting down trees and collecting materials to put up buildings, someday we may be able to do what nature does: Build structures from the bottom up.

Abalones, for instance, excrete a liquid that they use to make very tough shells. Wouldn't it be great if builders could do that, too? "Imagine pouring a liquid into a mold to assemble structures," Benyus says.

At a conference in the spring of 2004 in Minneapolis, Benyus encouraged architects and builders to make homes and other structures as beautiful as butterflies, as waterproof as beetle shells, as resistant to fire as redwood trees.

Nature provides the lessons. "There are amazing things right outside your door," she says. There's something new to learn from every living thing.

After Reading:

- Which possibility for nature-inspired invention mentioned in this article seems the most important to you? Why?

- Pick a biomimicry project you would like to take on. What animal or plant would you study? Why? How would you go about figuring out how to copy the desired quality?

- How would tiny bumps on the wings of a beetle help collect water? Draw a picture of how these bumps work. For additional information about the water-collecting beetle, see *http://news.nationalgeographic.com/news/2001/11/1101_desertbeetle.html* (*National Geographic*).

- Take a walk outside. Pick three plants or animals that you see and come up with something that humans could learn from each of them.

- In this article, many of the ideas that people want to copy from animals have to do with houses. Why do you think that is? What improvements would you like to see in your home? Could animals or plants suggest an answer to any of the problems that you see? Why or why not?

A New Way to Produce Energy

Over the years, scientists have come up with lots of ways to produce energy to run automobiles, appliances, and other machines, but most forms of fuel pollute the environment, can be expensive, and may eventually run out. In the following article, Emily Sohn takes a look at how the science projects of two bright teenagers uncovered new information about innovative fuels that may someday change the way we get our energy.

—The Editor

Boosting Fuel Cells

by Emily Sohn

Some people are happy to learn simply for the sake of learning. Megan Burger would rather use her education to create cutting-edge inventions with important uses.

That's exactly what the 18-year-old has done. At the 2005 Intel International Science and Engineering Fair (ISEF) in Phoenix, Arizona, the high school senior from The Woodlands, Texas, was one of several students who investigated fuel-cell technology. Her work might eventually help make Earth a cleaner place.

Fuel cells generate electricity through chemical reactions between hydrogen and oxygen. The process is an efficient way to produce energy with no toxic waste.

Fuel cells already power spacecraft and a few cars. In the future, experts suggest, they will also be used in homes and other buildings and even in devices such as laptops and cell phones.

The technology has "the potential to transform the [U.S.] energy industry," Megan says.

Still, there are problems. Even though there's more hydrogen in the universe than any other element, it's difficult to gather and store.

On Earth, most hydrogen is attached to oxygen (as in

111

water molecules, which contain two atoms of hydrogen for every atom of oxygen) or to other atoms, and energy is required to separate them. That's an issue if the point is to generate energy without the pollution produced by burning gasoline, oil, coal, and other fuels used today, which might be needed to free up hydrogen.

STRONGER, SAFER

For her project, Megan wanted to create a fuel cell that would be stronger and safer than those now available.

First, she did a lot of background reading, using books and the Internet, just to understand the basics of such a complicated topic. "I had to do a lot of research," she says.

One of the first things Megan learned is that a fuel cell has three main parts that fit together like a sandwich. The "bread" on one side is called an anode. The other slice of "bread" is called a cathode. The "meat" squished between the cathode and the anode is called an electrolyte. There are lots of different types of fuel cells, which differ mainly in the kinds of electrolytes they use.

In her experiments, Megan worked with a type of fuel cell called a solid-oxide fuel cell (SOFC), which has a solid electrolyte. SOFCs, which are stronger and safer than liquid versions, are used today in power plants, and engineers are looking for ways to use them in laptops and cell phones, Megan says. The downside is that they require high temperatures—around 1,000 degrees Celsius [1,832°F]—to work. This limits where the fuel cells can be used.

"I thought maybe I could make them operate at lower temperatures," Megan says.

For two years, Megan experimented with various electrolyte materials to lower the temperature at which an SOFC operates. Eventually, she ended up with solid pellets of a material called bismuth strontium barium oxide. No one had ever used this material before in a fuel cell, she says. Her tests showed that a fuel cell based on that material would be able to operate at a mere 650 degrees Celsius [1,202°F].

"That's already 350 degrees [662°F] less than before," Megan says. "It gives me hope that we can have another step down."

Her research continues. In the meantime, she has already learned more than she ever expected to learn— and not just about fuel cells.

"One of the biggest lessons is perseverance," she says. "If you want to find something exciting, you have to keep trying, no matter how many things around you are breaking, exploding, or not working. Thousands of things that people call failures are still things you can learn from."

COLD START

ISEF participant Wade Miller learned some important lessons from his fuel cell project, too. And like Megan, Wade didn't know where he was going to end up when he began.

"It was really confusing when I first started learning about it," says Wade, a 17-year-old senior from Albert Lea, Minnesota. Still, the concept was exciting enough to keep him going.

Because Wade lives in Minnesota, a state with hot summers and cold winters, he wanted to test a fuel cell's ability to withstand temperature extremes. His main goal was to figure out whether cars powered by fuel cells might some day be practical where he lives.

Unlike Megan, Wade used a polymer electrolyte membrane (PEM) fuel cell. These types of fuel cells work at relatively low temperatures, and they use sheet-like electrolytes that resemble plastic wrap.

To test efficiency at various temperatures, Wade built a toy car and attached a PEM fuel cell to it. That way, he could measure how much energy the cell produced. He tested the system under heat lamps at 80 degrees F [27°C], indoors at 65 degrees F [18°C], outdoors at 27 degrees F [-2.8°C], and in the school's freezer at -10 degrees F [-23.3°C].

Wade had predicted that the fuel cell would work best

at higher temperatures. Instead, it produced the most electricity at -10 degrees F.

"I ended up proving myself completely wrong," he says. "If you start a car in Minnesota when it's really cold, it takes a while for the engine to turn over. I thought the fuel cell would do the same. But I guess not."

In the end, Wade concluded that fuel cell-powered cars would run just fine in Minnesota. Still, he predicts, it'll be another 10 or 15 years before we actually see them on the streets.

"This is probably something we will deal with in the future," he says. "It's a good thing to get into. We will be seeing this in the news."

And today's young scientists are already on the case. As usual, taking a walk around the exhibition hall at the ISEF was like taking a walk into the future.

Glossary

abalones: Rock-clinging mollusks that have a flattened shell with a slightly spiral form.

attention-deficit/hyperactivity disorder (ADHD): A psychological disorder marked by disruptive behavior and problems with learning or concentration.

autopilot: A device for automatically steering ships and aircraft.

biodegradable: Able to be broken down by the actions of living things.

computer-mediated communication (CMC): Any form of communication between individuals through the use of separate computers or the Internet.

corrosion: Gradually wearing away through chemical processes.

drag: A slowing force that acts on an object moving through the air.

fuel cells: Devices that change the chemical energy of a fuel substance and an oxidant into electrical energy.

Global Positioning System (GPS): A system of navigation that uses satellite signals to determine the location of a radio receiver that is on or above the surface of the Earth.

glucose: A form of sugar used as energy by the body.

hybrid: Using a combination of gas and electricity as fuel.

hypersonic: Refers to speed that is five or more times faster than the speed of sound in air.

latitude: Distance north or south of the equator.

longitude: Distance between a given place and the prime meridian (located in Greenwich, England).

mollusks: Invertebrate animals with soft, unsegmented bodies usually enclosed in a shell.

pigments: Substances that produce color.

polymer: A chemical compound made up of repeating structural units.

proteins: Natural substances made of amino acid residues held together by peptide bonds.

scramjet: Aircraft in which the combustion of the fuel air mixture takes place at supersonic speeds.

solar wind: Plasma that comes off the surface of the sun and moves through space.

spectrometer: An instrument used to measure wavelengths of light.

supersonic: Faster than the speed of sound.

vaccines: Preparations of killed or weakened pathogens intro-
duced into the body to help create antibodies and provide pro-
tection against the pathogen in the event of later exposure.

virtual reality: An artificial environment experienced through
sensory stimuli provided by a computer.

Books

Ackroyd, Peter. *Escape From Earth*. New York: DK Publishing, 2003.

Baker, Christopher W. *Virtual Reality: Experiencing Illusion*. Brookfield, CT: Millbrook Publishing, 2000.

Bortz, Fred. *Techno-matter: The Materials Behind the Marvels*. Minneapolis: Twenty-First Century/Millbrook Press, 2001.

Jefferis, David. *Internet: Electronic Global Village*. New York: Crabtree Publishing, 2002.

Parker, Steve. *20th Century Media: 1990s, Electronic Media*. New York: Gareth Stevens, 2002.

Skurzynski, Gloria. *Are We Alone?* Hanover, PA: National Geographic, 2004.

Websites

Academy of Model Aeronautics
http://www.modelaircraft.org/

Biomimicry
http://www.biomimicry.net/

Biorobotics Laboratory, University of Washington
http://brl.ee.washington.edu/Research_Active/Exoskeleton/Exoskeleton_Index.html

DARPA Grand Challenge
http://www.darpa.mil/grandchallenge/index.html

Discovery Young Scientist Challenge
http://school.discovery.com/sciencefaircentral/dysc/

Integrated Media Systems Center: Virtual Classroom
http://imsc.usc.edu/news/virt_class_news.html

Life in the Atacama
http://www.frc.ri.cmu.edu/atacama/

NanoKids (Rice University)
http://nanokids.rice.edu/

NASA Ames Research Center
http://astrobiology.arc.nasa.gov/

The Planetary Society
http://planetary.org/solarsail/

Trademarks

Band-Aid is a registered trademark of Johnson & Johnson; Ritalin is a registered trademark of Novartis Pharmaceuticals; Spider-Man is a registered trademark of Marvel Characters, Inc.; Velcro is a registered trademark of Velcro Industries B.V.

Index

page:

EMILY SOHN is a freelance journalist, based in Minneapolis. She covers mostly science and health for national magazines, including *U.S. News & World Report, Health, Smithsonian,* and *Science News.* Emily divides her time between writing for kids and writing for adults, and assignments have sent her to countries around the world, including Cuba, Peru, and Sweden. When she's not working, Emily spends most of her time rock climbing, camping, swimming, exploring, and pursuing adventures outdoors.

TARA KOELLHOFFER earned her degree in political science and history from Rutgers University. Today, she is a freelance writer and editor with ten years of experience working on nonfiction books for young adults, covering topics that range from social studies and biography to health and science. She has edited hundreds of books and teaching materials, including a history of Italy published by Greenhaven Press. She lives in Pennsylvania with her husband, Gary, and their dog and cat.